THE EXTASIE

JOHN GALLAS was born in New Zealand in 1950. He came to England in the 1970s to study Old Icelandic at Oxford and has since lived and worked in York, Liverpool, Upholland, Little Ness, Rothwell, Bursa, Leicester, Diyarbakır, Coalville and Markfield, as a bottlewasher, archaeologist and teacher. He is the editor of two books of translations – *52 Euros* and *The Song Atlas* – and ten previous collections of his own poetry, all published by Carcanet. He is a Fellow of the English Association and was 2016 Orkney St Magnus Festival poet.

The
EXTASIE

JOHN GALLAS

CARCANET

First published in Great Britain in 2021 by
Carcanet
Alliance House, 30 Cross Street
Manchester M2 7AQ
www.carcanet.co.uk

A CIP catalogue record for this book is
available from the British Library.

ISBN 978 1 80017 085 8

Book design by Andrew Latimer
Printed in Great Britain by SRP Ltd, Exeter, Devon

The publisher acknowledges financial
assistance from Arts Council England.

CONTENTS

One

Two

THE EXTASIE

Mikey

ONE

THE BIRTHS OF LOVE

Begin
      issue of a stout-slung sperm,
I went like clockwork till you came: unfruitful,
soft-mechanic and Blind Man's Buff.

When I arrived (at nothing yet, because
it was not you), a small gold sovereign of small account,
ignorant of its kingdom and its currency,

I took you for a subject with my little fist,
banking on some notion, some credit on the unspent air,
drawn in an IOU, and showed you, unborn, mine.

In the end you came while I was busy,
long bones slipping out up to your eyes,
whose bulging shiners each bore my stamp,

minted in my mewling, hand-fast game.
All set then: though we knew, we had not met.
While twenty years of sturdy detour

took the necessary way to love, I did
some things of little profit, little note and little worth,
as notice to your solvency made flesh,

and things to come. I knew that I would profit well,
but not yet how, from your impression lent,
now you were not nothing anymore.

And I surprised you at first sight in Summer's
matching Snap, with liquid coin, which was
our fortune: to weep, recognising wonder.

FREEDESTINATION

So say we had no choice: that we were made
with holes each other's sizes, absences
the shapes of things to come,
to steer the star-coursed ship as if we did,
and pick our fated ends,
which are the hearts' intent.

So come on, let's try our proofs again,
and argue out, in beastly type,
their published, faint philosophies:
come on, let's press again our Complete Works
to sound the sheeted plagiary of Heaven
with tenses, both the doing and the done.

So say we prove both sides, and double find,
when I fit you, and you are all full-filled.

PAPERBOY

I rack my brain by stock and stook
to write your athanasic Rights;
I drag Invention up and down
clod and farrow bump bump bump
to ink you into Permanence: and I rehearse,
behind dull harvest's curtained fog,
the lines that make you Famous, and not die.

But I forget; things break
in sheaves and sheets of glass;
and all my writing runs
to wet and wander.

You are my paper and my news,
inked and foolscap-white; my rhyme and reason;
the long, delivered volume
in my hands I know by heart;
the work I read and write
at once; my study come to light.

SLEEP'S GEOGRAPHY

I wait at the navel of my world,
my ear laid on its middle march.

A quiet thump of Evolution
jogs the long white country.

Ssh, this is our hylic night,
when atlases embody, billow slow,

and bulge, and breathe –
I lift my sleepy head

and discover north,
then south. Here lie

Entelechy, Balnibari, Gaaldine,
Nihilon, Lothlorien and Farfelu,

whose scapes, like children's beaches,
mantle with some bright,

familiar dream,
and lantern-warm.

Give me all this lying, and these lands,
whose only business slumbers in my hands.

FIT FOR GLASSES

They kindly meant: one protested coy
I looked like *Owls at Evening.*
What was that about?

And fussed and fluttered over
little screws and hinges, this and that:
I did not need their consolation.

Now the farther world goes blurry;
what lies close is clear. Good.
Now I can concentrate on you.

And each correction of my dying senses
keeps your beauty, now machine-made, bright,
contracting all the world into our love.

So evening comes: I look down from my perch
at your sweet ecstasy with one beady eye,
my head a little sideways turned for clarity.

UNCONSCIOUS OF IT

You sleep too much: but then Outside
has never been your favourite place.
Now I sit up and watch the world for you.

The squirrel in his scoop of wood,
the lion in his oven, silly, soft Koalas
and the pointless Bat are your Taxonomy:

while I, the craning, scrupulous Giraffe,
swing my sight from left to right
in anxious perturbation, and in love.

Sleep, sleep on, for wake is worry:
there is time enough for that, when you will ride
disquiet and the world, and I sleep in.

CHRISTMAS IN HOSPITAL

The road from Thistleton is dark. Oaks
fling throes of blackerness among
the moonslapped rack.

They reckon God was born tonight.
Hedges, berries, beet-tops, thorns, uplift
their fatal fever, and beseech.

And died for us: impaled somewhere
tonight in Witham Wood, berries, thistles
and holly round his hair.

And everything is white and still with you,
nailed with cannula to a rood bed where
they keep the world alive,

labouring to deliver its eternity
and quiet-lighten all our nights.
I have laid my heart

at the foot of something:
a dripping yew,
a long light.

THE AIR BETWEEN

Sometimes we part perforce: I drive away
to some unlovely lot, some fallowland
that isn't you; you to Nod or
No Man's Land, and all the air between.

I stop at Prickwillow. From here to you
is just a hundred miles. The little Lark
laps slow as Sunday, all the world to round again.
I eat an apple in the dark, and rattle on.

Faster than the lick of Light, the Boffins say,
the universe expands, and I believe them. Ah,
love, I feel it now, tonight: they know.
At Shingle Street acceleration warps above the sea.

And so, you see, by Relativity, we approach
each other while we part, impetuous,
inevitable like small, sweet moons upon
the backs of worlds, which we to each other are.

OLD HUNSTANTON BEACH

Down here all's dark. Even we, each other's fires,
button up in one shared coat
to walk along the edge.

The sea's a sound; whose thrumming giants
generate just breath; whose moonbeams stink
of iodine; whose gulls are gusts.

I know the stars are dead: I read it somewhere:
that their lights are letters
posted while they lived.

We cross the big blue page with gapen mouths.
And then we disappear, two Is but blind,
way down the line and shore.

But still our radiation and remains,
cradled through these million years, will sure re-light
the correspondence of some silent sun.

ONCE WE STAMMERED

Barrelling through Barons Court
I bit the corners off my Pass
and slyly stared around the comely beauts.

Bouncing thus in this fair company,
I saw him smile, I saw him rise,
I saw the glory in his eyes –

who said:
Weep for Adonais, he is dead,
Charlie is me darling,
Nymphs and Shepherds, come away,
I was cured of my stammer today.

Wow. We freight of folk
rattled under Hammersmith:
and someone cried *Ay-men!*

and some said *Yes*, and some said *Bless,*
and some were dumb, but shone: and then
he sat down again.

And silent I said:
Ample make this Bed,
Now yiz are in the Willingdone Museyroom,
Far from the madding crowd's ignoble strife,
so, love, you have cured me of the stammer of my life.

WHEN WITH FLESHLY BRIDGES...

When with fleshly bridges we are joined,
and revving up the road to Shakers End
and Rekareka's Do & Dance,
love, how could we mind
what we have left behind?

Who needs a map to find your heart ? What cones,
what signs could route me swifter to your quick?
What wipers and what lights
could make things clearer?
What engine steer us nearer?

And when the dazzle and the horn are done,
the home road run, the idle bridges down,
and we are soft with sleep,
ah, shut the door,
our fit behind us, and the world before.

OPERATION ALL SAINTS, EAST NORTON

I see by this, the Thankful Window,
that they all came home.
Thank God for that:

the orange words are leached
with sun-clot now, and beam
their happy Triumph in Belief.

Tonight you lie in No Man's Land,
gassed and sick, and slit with steel:
and I am here... I know

that they are all dead now: so may I have
the Hope and Heat that raised this glass,
and see you walking home.

GEDNEY DROVE END

I made a Poet, because I like it here,
who haunts the Wash, and dies of Love (with sheep):

and he betrays me. Twice, along Marsh Lane,
lost in rhymes of his, my bike

has bucked me down to bleed among
its slubbered blebs and ruts:

these crashing scabs and goffered bruises bear
ouched witness to his black, ungrateful spite.

A pack of pink-foot geese slip through the scud:
freighters rust in distant drizzle.

I sit on the bank, and I am him. Poor Isaiah.
See how my own imagination harms me.

To this unhappy labour, to this red,
spindrifted birth that bites the brain

and bone that make it, I turn (with sheep)
because I am not occupied with you.

BRANCASTER BEACH

What luck of plans or planets brings us here
exactly at the turning of the tide;
to see the first wee bubble-back,
the first-oozed runnel run?

The sea, in little sleeves, arrives.

We sit amongst the dunes and ask your phone:
in fact, it is The Moon,
librating from its Apogee,
and nought to do with us.

The sun wakes on its duty.

We watch the sheets and sway slide
through the ghosts of our soles.
Redshanks splish and pick.
We share our freezing hands.

Dispassionate coincidence: enjoy.

DID I NEVER HAVE A SOUL...

Did I never have a soul,
or had I it *removed*
by some contorted order
and a fork?

I am not occupied
with immortal longings.

You are my Pantheon:

whose sweet proscriptions
took on tablets
blank as placeboic psalms
only give me ease –

from argument, and all
the dark philosophies of fear.

You are my Laws and Acts.

Midnight. I lean on the window,
a candle in my hand,
the watchman of our lives.
Heaven shimmers high.

Who needs its long, conditional bliss?
It cannot be lovelier than this.

You are my Seraphim.

Put off your soul like any Saint,
but not the sleeping skin
that makes the book,
your mystery all over it.

And you stream plain light
from any sheet and shroud.

You are my Testaments.

TAKING YOUR PART

I'll play Foul Misfortune,
huddled hooded
on the Quarry bank,
broken alexanders
and a view of cranes

because the part possesses you.

Anyway, I'll sit down in the mud,
it suits me for a while:
my brother-cast,
clamouring in tongues
and books of verse,

attend me now:

King Gaol, with his chest of bars,
Master Car Crash, with his bootless steering wheel,
Sir Sickness, with his knife and needle bright,
Doctor Dole, pent up in sellotape, and

Lord Delay and Worry, the ruffed and frantic sluggard.

And I'll exit by a shorting moon,
when footlights come to custom's constellations:
how unwillingly the understudy
gives up to the star.
We never close.

Take back your stage and wow it.

And I am weary back to me again,
huddled hooded
on the Quarry bank,
broken alexanders
and a view of cranes,

the acting friend of love.

ON STANTON FIELDS

Here, the hedges *bristle.* Bosky blades burst
swording at the sky. And from the general womb
of earth its flagged army shoulder-stones into the field.

The sun provokes. The air extracts. How surely Spring is sprung.

This little, ranty daisy, see, blundering
to snatch existence with its petal-fist upon
a ram of glaucous flesh, will do well enough to figure

this, the world's renewed attack, which you have made on me.

No room. No room. Let fail and fall the contents of
my last years' arms before this green, and occupy,
and overthrow, erupt in your advance, unsheathe from me,

whose Wintertime I was, and whose Summer I will be.

WORK

What I finished, you began.
Behind the hedged trees you dig for me.
The busy spade : the levelled floor:
the long dark house: the empty door.

O promise, love, when you still work,
but I will never go again,
to wind me in your winding-shirt
and dig me in the quiet dirt.

Build your house behind the trees:
make my pate the pantry bed,
make my ribs the study pan,
and end what I began.

POEM ON A BIKE

I found a word-worm in my brain:
its knotty line was you.
Precious, therefore, I tried
to keep it safe with repetition,
pedalling it to permanence
come hill, come bunt, come hours that die
and blanch invention out.

Comes the bastard hill anon,
and comes the bastard rain:

and then a scary rattle-down,
which-while I chanted off
our sentence yet at forty miles an hour,
a-bounce and slap but keeping still,
quite still, that gimballed bowl
of level sense
wherein lay all my cause.

Comes the happy end eventual,
and comes the happy biro.

And so this came, exact,
whose perfect faults daunt me not,
who carried it still harping in his skully ark,
not loosed to luck or loveliness,
whose coupled words have reached
forgiven land, and live,
and which I could not bear to change, like you.

Comes the sweet worm ideal,
comes sweet incorruption so.

SLEEP & BE DONNE

Come to bed, and after that
that Master John call Extasie
we'll sleep like spoons
past all the shorter dark of Spring.

And laid against each other's bowls
within this bolstered drawer, sometimes
we'll turn like two
made one, and kiss, and sleep anew.

While in our draughty cupboards sit
our matched and mettled souls like cups
that overflow
and yet are still, and hearken so

at one another that they seem
each other's glass, where, dead and bright,
they hold us in
harmonical oblivion.

A WALK AWAY

I stopped to piss into a grove of silence.
Buttercups reached my flies; cow parsley
unruffled still on six-foot stalks; and limelush grass
packed in lighted cushions, too fat to fall.

Longer than need be, I hung around,
rooted in superfluous eternity: not high,
broad, deep, or timely – only all intent
in this bright-quiet, spire-stemmed minstrelsy

forever on the edge of song: its breath
all drawn, and the note believed. Mine too,
held inside-out : that this I did not want to leave,
as it became you, love, my only equal to its all.

A FEAR OF SOMETHING AFTER DEATH

Some folks (who do not know, but still) allow
a lively Second Life to be
endured, undead and endless, after this;

whose prancing wardrobes' work, whose bastard bliss
would leach our merry suit to seem
the pallid shift of universal love.

Leave well enough alone. And yet, because
you are my soul, which of itself
is motley mortal free, I'll raise again
the buried flesh of promise and desire

to know you in the ghastly, ghostly fire
at Christ's damnable clambake, clothed
in purple wounds amongst the closet-white,
my ecstasy usurped, my lust dismayed.

WHEN I STRIDE ALONG

When I stride along
the foot of Hillside Hay
the nearest wheatstalks rattle briskly by; while they,
more bluey-green, half-yonder up the swelling slope, go
more slow, a sort of moderate-passing flow; and where the
hornbeam crowns the ridge, the distant harvest *inches* out perspective's hub.

It still moves.

I guess, by all the laws of *Ocular Kinetics*, there must be a fixed point,
extrapolate-behind, where you, nest-curled in moss, still-silent lie
amidst the earth, which roundabout revolves
in tiers of speed, from Thought to Ecstasy,
from my poor measure,
even to the stars.

B.L. EGERTON 2711: SIR THOMAS WYATT'S POEM-BOOK

If I understand your dapper hand,
you pine for love: though nothing new,
it's woven well. I lean and look.

My fever here I see
shuttled back to me
from the loom-thread of your book.

I leave on the looking-glass
a butter-film reflected of
my brother-brow.

Tonight, in the lowered library light,
we will spin a tale upon a sigh,
Sir Thomas and I.

THE MONUMENT

What pink philosophers, snagged in thought,
could argue now that I am not in love?

What course, what plan, what atomies of mind,
what argument, what school of sense, what reason
could now advance its epagogic army
against my feeble power?

What pointed weapons dipped in proof
dismantle all the body of my belief?

What canon butt me now? What spectacle
of strategy surprise my private troop,
and ambush my affections as they wander,
scattered and incapable as clouds?

What bright ideas replace the sweet
dark glasses of my dreams?

Yesterday I fell asleep in you, and when I woke
upon the quiet field of war, my modest monument
still stood, in witness to my happy blindness,
ignorant and warm within.

THE RAVENS

I saw two ravens
squirt out of the earth
who looked like Love.

In savage flight
they snapped the lightened band
above the wheat

and trampled up beyond
its fond, still-green convention
to eat the bright, cold air.

THE SUFI SHEEP

Here comes the sheep,
to see the curious length
of twisted ease inside her fence:

who looks at me across
her big bone bridge of snout
so long and still I ask,

what do you think of me?
I think of Love, she says.

Her bugwet eyeballs
wander on to all the thorns and nettles
hot and sad beside the road.

Everything, she says, wrapt
beyond her popgun droppings,
makes me think of Love.

Other sheep sleep, fubsy-stale,
as if on stairs, up the shaven hill.

NIUE

I like to think you'd like it here,
far from the old grey hemisphere:
our love lies not in thought – it is a kind
of hot blue sky of the mind.

Enreefed with sharp sufficiency,
upreared of careless fires, we,
abstruseless in our wrapt and glittered space,
seem fit for such a place.

LANGARY GATE, OCTOBER EVENING

How short of level Lincolnshire,
green and brown
under the late, low sun,
falls all the company of men:

this hour I'm in, for instance, flat
as drovers' drink,
whose still content outwells
all the gingerbeer of happiness

but you – my company of one,
slowsap and root
of all my level lands,
lapped in long, late, low sun.

BOMBING PRACTICE

The red flag's up at Dawsmere Wash:
here come the planes. I sit atop
the blotted levee
and suck a pint of milk.

Hulks and bulwarks, orange-primed
and fat with salt, hold their breaths,
unsuspect as usual,
along this run of wrack.

And now, like hauled zips, the planes
un-tooth the sky, attended, after,
by their cries,
and scattered larks, and light.

And all the dull, hydroptic land
returns in clods and ochre slob,
and the shot ships
settle like cows in the mud.

The wind returns with plaited cloud,
the birds go up again;
my milk, quite turned,
lumps the grass with curds.

The flag comes down. The towers drop
their sunlit blinds. The tide retires.
I recognise
the dinning charge of love.

THE LITTLE LEAF THAT WOULD NOT FALL

At Potters Field the oaks
are shutting down, and drop their plashy
batteries round my Fallen Troopers.

Here I am amid the leaves
to pluck the common meaning
from their fall: *but this one won't* –

whose paper curl stays level-lifted
up beside my eyes, still in the air
and yellow-light.

As lovers say (and so we are)
that wonder's best, I quickly leave
this leafy extasie airborne and alone.

The woods are wild today
and rot and drop: yet we, love,
for a wonder, do not decay.

HORSE-EYE, FOX, AND CROW

This black globe
invests my ogling landscape
in its glass – bright and fat
crook-trees, cankers, clouds:

the fox that follows
turns into the hawthorn
with my thinking cap
and takes it tawn to the woods:

the bird that sits still as a nightmare
pinned with bodkin branches
on a rackbacked oak
considers my dust:

but you, who keep all figures of myself,
return my interest tenderly,
and cross reflection's reach
to close me in your arms.

LEARNING CLOUDS

I stood on a foolscap of snow at Markfield Field,
and marked the Clouds out of my book
(that is the *Cirrus* yonder, speeled
atop the pylons; and that is the *Cumulus,*
a wintry roil dabbed in pink ; and that
is the *Stratus,* phlegmish, flush, and flat)

as if the Word came first, and then the sky
condensed the abstracts of Its will.
I crackled home. The sun was shy.
The day was short. I echoed out the names:
and underneath the naked birch my world
precipitated, pat – the herled

milk-lines in your second nail; the fat
dough-rise of your scar; the quires
and reams of fingerbone; the flat,
noctilucent iris of one eye.

These heavens. And these books. What can I do,
when all I learn, I learn as you.

A WHALE IN BORROWED SMALLS

Whilst you bled
in Lincoln Gaol
I saw a whale,

slubbered on the sand at Thornham Marsh,
and rotting in a wind-ripped noon.
It stank: it had a winking eye.

There is a kind of patience in the flesh
of we who live; and if the fact is fled,
what tardy mountain-multitude of cells

still silent shrink
their age away,
bloodless day by bloodless day.

A snapping ring of murder-tape
makes private our too long decay.
Well, there is comfort in your shorts.

Take the fond forbearance, then,
this marvellous monster needs no more
to entertain you: I will hurry on

to Titchwell and the farm,
and stride over the giant,
cutten fields, my head among

the winded squads of geese,
to keep from lumpen despair
the occupation of your underwear.

5.26 FROM LINCOLN

I left You in the care of god, though I care not for him.

The cold cold train pulls out over High Street.
Bundled folk look in.

Above, his million tons of light
floats unreasonably in the night,
and I am let believe.

Dear unwonted flying object,
hover near my Love awhile,
which may be there and everywhere,
and make Him smile.

And in my sleep to Burton Joyce
the prayer of my pragmatic choice
turns the ship of heaven east,
like some bright throng-decked saint hotel,
and blinds the Lover in his cell.

AND IF YOU WATCH...

And if you watch me sleep
as I do sometimes you, one elbow piered
up on the pillow, peering at
my little trial of death,
then make of me, love,
what you will:

my skull your winter cap,
my ears your shoes,
my blindness for a sail;
my toppled cock a nail,
my breath the blues,
my thumb your watch-strap.

And if you watch me still,
as I do sometimes you, make the log
I sleep like, love, your bere and prop
and take me bitwise in, and summon me
until I am your sum and whole
and have no cause to wake.

TODAY I CHOKED...

Today I choked
on my own happiness,

which seemed a too-much meal,
and someone else's share,

brought me where I walked
on a cold white winter plate:

eight hopping crows
in a lemon freeze;

the sun's cracked plunge,
its white eye sat
upon some hedges'
bright argental shore;

new-slashed slopes of hedgerow,
thorn-runes, glass and nail;

the song, after, of the slow tractor
shattering shreds;

and this I threw up slap
in Loddington Lane

beside three gawp-snout sheep,
hot, on the frost, in a happy heap.

HIGHER DARWINISM

We are the Barnacles of Heaven, you and I:
the tardy-bearded origins
of betterment by Love.

Our clamminess proceeds to crabs:
which is our Habit, so entire
that friends and fish connive.

It is our Reason : convivial examples of
proofs in pink, complete and shown,
commendable as urchins.

And all the little oysters sit,
their lessons learned, about our knees,
tiny pearls upon their tongues.

And our Belief, whose actual awe
and study of each other, which we are,
recommends our Species to a star.

LOVER IN A STORM

I walked in the wood, and the wind
slapping my shoelatches.
Oak-boughs bounced at the cold
jellies of my eyes. Holly-hedges
rattled like buckshot:
but I was not.

Swish and swosh the grass,
thrashing at the boisterous sky.
Crows, pricked by turning feathers,
beat at whirlabout. The shreddy nettles
black-rotted in the rain:
but I did not complain.

These passionate mechanics moved
their pictures on a screen of cloud.
Something over-knotted my laces.
Furrows piped in the fields.
The crows cracked umbrella wings:
but I was moved by other things.

PORTRAIT OF GIOVANNI GEROLAMO GRUMELLI – 'THE MAN IN PINK'

I stand and stare, and there *you* are:
not in some chiming match or measure,
some echo of your shape or size,
but something sounder, and Otherwise.

He has not your hand, nor you his eyes:
under the Candy-Ponce what shoulder
or what cock, or, understill, what heart
or stepping-stones of spine, remains just Art.

But triple-deep I know *that* Mr. G,
like this one of more modest frame,
would bow, and blush, and rattle, meeting you,
acknowledging his Otherwise, as I do.

LOVE & SONS

Love & Sons, I am your Printing Press:
the old, quadruple-chambered Business where
the repetitious thumping of old news
is thought abroad, in extasies and ink.

What profits it ? Our smiles are not the Sun's;
our eyes make not a Mirror to the world;
our Echo and our Times, whose lines commute
the sentence of our souls, unneighboured stand

in a Springing field in Lincolnshire, and rattle
like a windmill at the sky. Outside
the earth is blue, and busy crows rewrite
their automatic wonder in the air.

And I have battered out the last bright saws
of love ; and I am set and dry; and
pause.

TWO

THE HEARTSEASE

Jesus Christ, I'm sitting on a weed
in Bedlam Field
staring at a Heartsease in a slub

under a muffled drum of clouds.

Ha, I am not Mad John, or not Despised,
Rejected, oh
contrariwise, I am too much in love. And so

I sit with Johnny Jump-Up in the dark.

I roundly-wipe my glasses, and lean more close to this
dear, honest plant,
whose flowerless braid of winter greens

dangles in a ring of thorns.

The crisscross stem is bowed and pale
from thirsty tire;
the hearty leaves, in glossy slump, waggle wet
in the wind their tiny, bickered teeth.

Which is enough of That. My pants are plashed,
my fingers pricked:
but I have done my duty: see, the cloud rolls

slowly now upon a cylinder of light.

I take too long on you. I only thought
to balance back
the World itself by paying it some

holy-wrapt attention. Which I have done.

THE GOOSE

I saw a fat and lonely goose
labour to the quarry edge,
so low, she nearly took my cap
to wheeze in. Then she dipped into the pit.

I waited. Just a leaden loom of sky,
treetops, and a falling field.

But happy men have happy hearts
to hazard on a Goose's Tale:

I saw a braw and bonny bird
at her elastic odyssey,
in timely kind, and near-above,
who found, and landed on, her love.

TOWARDS THE BLACK HOLE

It's Autumn and I'm cold.
The mortal brilliance of a wall of leaves
accelerates fire as I drive

the old white carcass down to Spinney Hill.
The sun is setting. I am only atoms, after all,
hauled and haled towards the night-maw

whose black event is one horizon past
my dalliance of days. I buy a box of batteries.
The tide of rowan-flame frets besides

while I rattle home. I wind the windows down.
Brightening like a dish of fire carried
up the road, I think of you.

The sun, its forehead wreathed in flame, goes out.
I'll show them I can burn before I'm gone:
that I was accounted yours, and shone.

UNLEARNING A VIEW

The cargo sidles in to Westray dock.
Over the sides sheerwaters stitch the sea-carpet.
We are the only passengers. No one leaves.

Drizzle shifts under a cloud of light.
The ship-crane lands plastic drainpipes.
And there, behind the rounds of rope,

sits Grim, wagging his flea-shot beard,
in a blue cape-hood, waiting with an axe
for Cousin Kjetil to come, and piss his life away.

Look, you said at something
and suddenly I do, along the shore-road,
winking, in the wind-wheel and the rain:

a line of vans with their back doors open;
folks in sweaters waiting;
and a store-shed roofed with stippled silver.

PSALM 102

I wonder what the witless owl
does, crying in the dark
boo-hoot boo-hoot for love.

It kneads at an empty waste, dismayed,
where no trees grow. Can't it fly?
I have finished this Psalm.

Ah, you are not my shipwreck's raft,
nor I your airbag; but at common
roost we call along

the bosky weald at brighter need,
to-wit to-woo, for love if not
deserved, at least allowed.

THE DEW-DROP

I tipped the kissing-gate in Bagworth Wood.
Its pewter latch went clonk. I morrissed through.
The reddled sun, Day's Knight's advancing shield,
flung wet glitter off the treetops.

The earth was all beset with thicket-mist.
I shut the gate, and with a neat back-turn,
stepped out of it: whereat, my passing nose
came up direct upon a Dew-drop

held out on a thorn-branch end, and so
exactly near I did not press one single atom
of its wee glass cushion, though we touched and stood,
nose, drop and thorn, in perfect triple-kiss

and quietude. At my back the gold device
splashed up through the steaming oaks.
Cross-eyed with syzygy, I peered – I had no choice –
into the globe, which took up flame,

and in its skin I saw my eye, and therefore you,
who are its whole possessor and delight
and pillowed me against the thorns of life, in quiet need;
and I did not bleed.

A VALEDICTION OF MY FACE, IN A WINDOW

This phizog is starting to piss me off.
Galleries of every glass hang the grey old master
at its self: here, there, at every turn
I look away
in dull dismay.

Can't I be for once a picture newly done;
with lamb-white paint; in groovy style; tomorrow
when the umpteen dioptric shades
that double me
re-trouble me?

Ah, but you have bought it, love, liking,
for a wonder, this long likeness;
and looking thus I see reflected
what you see,
which changes me.

TRAVELLING LIGHT

At long long last I came
at three o'clock,
nude as a fish
and bawling.

Amid my fucking furniture
I long to be light
again and make
good riddance.

The long house waits.
May I go to it weightless
except for you,
which is all I want.

NEWTON-IN-THE-ISLE

At four o'clock the February sky
let loose a sudden smatch
and shower like salt
shook once across the vittles of the land
I pedalled past from Tydd.

The sun lay low on Fitton End,
and all the watersides, and blinked
behind the shortling waft of white.
Newton next. The flooded fields like metal trays,
and nothing rode the road but I.

The village sign, six black boyos
in Transport Type on silver sheeting,
softly burst in blooms of light
back in my face, with all
the quiet clamour of a cloud.

A moment, then, it blossomed: then I passed.
Why invent the truth: my eyes are headlights,
dynamo'd with fierce content,
that spill some radiance that wakes
the retroreflect fire in everything.

I pedalled down the darkling street elate,
past the prettier sign,
on which Sir John and Mary in the Marsh,
the dull white lion rampant,
six hushed bells, and a weed of woad are painted

and sawn out on a pole: whose particular
and huddled history, to me,
was a mere Dark Age beside
the common guide, like a February island
laid in a sea of dazzle seasoned with rain.

THE BEARDED ANGELS OF NORTH CREAKE
CHURCH

You're in the English Elongated Style,
Late, and Horizontal, like these:
lean, wood-white and leaning down
from the creaking hammer-roof.

There's a wind outside
where the new daffodils slap;
but here in quietness I walk the aisle
holding a mirror like a tray of light:

and looking in, they pass above,
some with musick, some with beards,
watching in this high dark shell,
the hushed procession of my bones.

I stop: the windows rattle. Then return,
steady as a waiter. I put the mirror back.
Cold wind shakes the door; and I leave
this wooden heaven for a scimble of trees.

Inside, the mirror develops, in its silver
plate and pool, a picture of my passing:
the angels, sharpening and still,
inclining me, in your fashion, to endure.

I HAVE CHOSEN MY HEAVEN...

I have chosen my heaven
from the Catalogue of Lights:
Number 40172646,
Cold View of the Wash.

In it, the sky is long, and leaden-white.
The sea is way beyond the stretch of suck
and salted scurvygrass, samphire and blight.

While on the bank, two bolstered backs with arms
around each other's shoulders sit and seem
to stare the same somewhere. Behind, the farms

blurr their bladed ploughlines, and the cows
wait planted in the wind. Around this page
a reed-braid, empty as the air, soughs

at the dint of Death, His clapping-shears
not bent on execution, but to prune
these lovers, to grow stronger with the years.

So I have chosen this heaven
from the Catalogue of Lights:
Number 40172646,
Cold View of the Wash.

THE LAY OF THE LAND

Hot for June. Rolling out
of Allexton
the fields fret and bulge
their burning bulk.

A haunch of wheat threshes,
green and low, in warm unease:
the cud-and-cardboard reek
of beans spills off the banks:

and bine and nettles,
shouldered up
on wagging hedge-heads,
tangle with my wits.

Infatuate with heat and joy,
I enter by a private path
the sweating grounds.
You are the lay of the land.

82 DEGREES

Sheep shit in the shade.
The canal pops like hot jam.
Great oaks fan and faint.
The ruddle bridges burn.

Yet they know not desire.

I pass like Meshach herealong,
unbaked and cool, their fumerole,
blazes of dung-reek, bubble-grill
and hectic quercus, to the humpback flames.

Ah, they know not fire.

YOUR FEVER

Sick again. I sit in the dumps
and read The Lexicon of Plagues.

Round my ears the hot, loof greens
work their feast and fall without complaints;

whilst we, all fevered-full with sense,
are hounded by the guddler in our beds.

The quarry rattles dust. Chapter Four:
here, I hope, is Reason in the Works.

Neglect?
            No, no. I have your habits safe
hung up in the purple wardrobe of my heart.

Taboos?
            Hm. What we have done
has flourished me : and we are one.

A Feud?
            Ha! What energy remains
from Love's clash of arms for figs and foils?

Or Turpitude?
                Your neighbours have their cars,
and who would charge your pulling down the stars

for me? I shut the Lexicon, unpleased.
Bastard wig-wasps walk across my face.

The trucks heave out. Your fever cannot stay:
sleep it thoughtlessly away. The bucket-belts begin,

crish*crash*, crish*crash*. Perhaps it's best that we
are hunted, tickled by the self-same hand

that gave us all the fearful flight to live.
But, ah, it was a cruel thing to give.

BAGWORTH HEATH WOOD

A moot of Mother-die
droops under huge bronze crowns.

The oaks hold out their newborn scarlet hands.
The nettles are in yellow-fall and all the flags and rushes

suck the mummied earth, where small black
butterflies zip on the hot updraught.

I walk through. I am not needed
by the green performance of this round.

Birches flicker ; tiny stick-flies
stand pin-steel in the air, here, then there.

Past the clover-clotted meadows
the Bowl sits bald and silent-still.

I sit in the feathergrass. Here,
above this hard blue dip

red skylarks used to bubble up and blow.
For half a sixpence I

would sit in a desert and sing
in case some wanderer, passing by,

thought that birds were gone for good
from this enamoured Wood.

THE SANDALS OF T.E. LAWRENCE

A wormy dreamtime
bade me rise and go:
I rose and went.

Sure enough,
they were there:
the sandals of Mr Lawrence
slap-flat on the fuzzy floor
of an acrylic wardrobe,
dusted as windlestraw.

I glided forth and hooked on my Fendis.

Ha. Just what I saw in my sleep:
a hammock for the heel;
a strap for the dorsum;
a thong for the halluxean interstice.

The foot, of course, dead as a mummy.

Small blue and yellow quadratures
decorate the wider leatherings.
Or did I imagine that. I can't remember.

I hurried home, thrice-comforted.

That night, cosinuous as spoons,
we dropped off together,
and I did not think of the mysteries of the world.

Let them be mysteries, and make us smile.

Unshape the ship, and close your eyes;
we'll sail into the fond moon-shine,
and I will I hold your feet on mine.
You will do for all that means to me.
Sleep now, and let us see what we shall see.

WHO HIC SHOOT STAR?

On Berberis lawn,
a bottle in each hand,
necks on our backs,
we watch The Plow
slow-till its furrow
down the darkling sky.

In hushed,
mechanic pause
we gape,
then gulp.

See how the Plowboy,
each step an hour,
treads his cosmic measure
to drive his tralatitious share
amongst the thistle-stars.

Poplars girt
our little island-green,
night-shivery with silver business.
Glug glug.

We wobble closer.

Oh.

Two shooting stars.

A short totter, and down we go in the dew.
Haha. Splash.
Clink the bottles all.

Look, John, look:
celestial cows gallop to new grazing
Bobo spurts his seed at the Great Egg
the souls of the poor go home after dinner on Mars
the scimitar of Murphy
matakōkiri gift of fire
the bolts of Pinguin's War
Pahokatawa comes to say all's well
the common man flees before tyranny

and the general sprint.

Gulp.

You nod off with a big fat smile.
The poplars flitter.

Much more, much more,
I hope their fire is Physics,
and a bit of Maths:

some quantum-ish,
phenomenal
monotony
along some cold immensity –

which, rather neatly,
leaves the sky
hic
for *us* to occupy.

I hold your horizontal hand,
and watch our glowing bloom expand
like genies from their bottles
and the pale lamp of your face,
beyond the trees,
beyond the stars,
and into outer space.

CALF & HARE

Moon-Clarabelle against an oak:
she squirts her shiny sack

to the late lime stubble,
sunshot with September.

I hook my chin up on
the gate two bright hours long

stockstill and stare
while little Angus

wonders well what walking is
and how to take the air.

Then Hadley Hare
in madmaid's frolic

shoots sideways
out of a hedge

and off across
the wimbling wideness.

Once she stops to measure
where her sprinting space

will find the finish-line
of safer thorn.

And I walk on,
my Autumn story made,

The Calf and the Hare
and the Oak Above,

with all the childish innocence
of love.

THE STIR

The world is white: under a blank-penny sun
I pedal down the dingle past Dug the Donkey,
up to Slobland View, and out by Fortune's Field:

wide, long, thick with jackdaw-heads like stacked potatoes,
shut-eyed in the wind, that burble, fluff and jostle
as I roll my head along their height of hedge:

so they take off, and leave in one pitch-wave
my sweeping skull, peeling off the plough-striped counterpane
with caws of ecstasy, and up-dissolve away.

The night clock stares its silver coin at one a.m. –
I hear you bombling up the stairs, and lift the sheet away,
and wait to leave the common ground.

PLAN FOR OUR DEATH

On the long lane out of Hallaton
I spotted death
heading for someone else.

I pulled my head in
while he passed,
drawing a springe,

whose stock was cloud,
jaws were blasted beech,
and tarmac was his plate.

I asked if he would come for me, not yet
of course, when we were slept like spoons,
to save us all the waste of time.

His answer was a spookish draught
that loosed the last wytch-leaf along the tump,
and danced it in the dark.

TELEGRAM TANKA

The course of true love
is smooth as an angel's arse.
Should you run into
obstacles the chances are
that God is not involved.

Stop.

*